Write-and-Learn
Word Family
Practice Pages

SCHOLASTIC
PROFESSIONAL BOOKS

New York • Toronto • London • Auckland • Sydney • New Delhi
Mexico City • Hong Kong • Buenos Aires

Coordinated by Rebecca Callan
Cover design by Norma Ortiz
Cover and interior artwork by Jane Dipold and Rusty Fletcher
Interior design by Norma Ortiz

ISBN: 0-439-45876-5
Copyright © 2003 Scholastic Inc.
All rights reserved. Published by Scholastic Inc.
Printed in the U.S.A.

1 2 3 4 5 6 7 8 9 10   40   09 08 07 06 05 04 03

• Contents •

• Introduction •

Welcome to *Write and Learn Word Family Practice Pages*!

These ready-to-go pages introduce and reinforce 30 word-family patterns. They also ensure kids get lots of practice writing and reading many words within each featured word family—expanding children's vocabulary and strengthening automatic word recognition, a critical element for reading success.

Use the practice pages for whole-group, small-group, or individual work. You might also:

- give practice pages to children to complete at home

- put copies of the pages in a writing center

- have children create folders in which they collect their completed sheets and bind into a book when all the pages have been completed

- include the pages in children's portfolios

Using the Practice Pages

The practice page follows the same format and children may complete each page the same way.

In the Word Building section they:
- Put the letters together to make a word in the word family. Children might begin by saying the word aloud (so that they have an auditory experience as well as a visual one).

In the Sentence Fill-ins section they:
- Cut out the letters at the bottom of the page and glue them in the correct squares to complete each sentence. Doing this gives students a hands-on experience with word building and provides practice reading word family words.

In the Word Scramble section they:
- Unscramble each word and write it on the line.

In the Word Search section they:
- Find and circle each word from the word bank, discriminating between commonly confused letters and building faster word recognition.

In the More Words section they:
- Write a sentence using one or more words in the featured word family.

• How to Use This Book •

Procedures for Enhancing Word Family Practice

You might follow these steps for each word family:

1. Preview the word pattern (or phonogram) you will introduce by writing a few words within that family on the board or chart paper. Ask students to identify the phonogram the words have in common.

2. Invite students to think of words that rhyme with the word family. Write their ideas on the board or on chart paper. Together, determine which words are nonsense words and which words have different word patterns and do not belong in the word family the class is studying.

3. Have children "air trace" the phonogram in the air (so that students have a kinesthetic experience as well as an auditory and visual one).

4. Then give each child a practice page. (Consider completing one page together as a class activity.)

Word Families Grid

Use this grid to locate specific words covered in this book.

Phonogram	Word Families	Phonogram	Word Families
-ack	black, pack, sack, shack, snack, stack, tack, track	-ide	bride, glide, hide, pride, ride, side, slide, tide
-ail	frail, mail, pail, sail, snail, tail, trail, quail	-ight	bright, fight, flight, fright, knight, light, might, tight
-ain	brain, chain, drain, grain, pain, rain, train, stain	-ill	bill, chill, drill, grill, hill, quill, sill, will
-ake	bake, cake, fake, lake, make, rake, snake, take	-in	chin, fin, grin, pin, shin, spin, twin, win
-ale	bale, kale, pale, sale, scale, stale, tale, whale	-ine	line, nine, pine, shine, spine, swine, twine, vine
-an	bran, can, fan, man, pan, ran, than, van	-ing	king, ring, sing, sling, sting, string, swing, wing
-ank	bank, blank, crank, drank, plank, stank, tank, yank	-ink	drink, link, pink, rink, sink, stink, think, wink
-ap	cap, clap, gap, map, nap, sap, strap, wrap	-ip	chip, drip, flip, grip, rip, ship, snip, trip
-ash	cash, crash, flash, mash, rash, sash, splash, trash	-ock	clock, dock, flock, knock, lock, rock, smock, sock
-at	bat, cat, chat, flat, hat, rat, sat, spat	-op	chop, cop, crop, hop, mop, shop, stop, top
-ay	bay, clay, fray, gray, hay, jay, sway, tray	-ot	cot, hot, knot, pot, shot, spot, tot, trot
-ell	bell, fell, sell, shell, smell, spell, well, yell	-uck	buck, cluck, duck, luck, puck, stuck, truck, tuck
-est	best, chest, nest, pest, rest, test, vest, west	-ug	bug, dug, hug, jug, mug, plug, snug, tug
-ice	dice, mice, nice, price, rice, slice, spice, twice	-ump	bump, dump, grump, hump, jump, plump, pump, stump
-ick	chick, kick, lick, pick, sick, slick, thick, trick	-unk	bunk, dunk, hunk, shrunk, skunk, stunk, sunk, trunk

Word Family Activities

At the end of this book you'll find reproducible pages that can be used for practice:

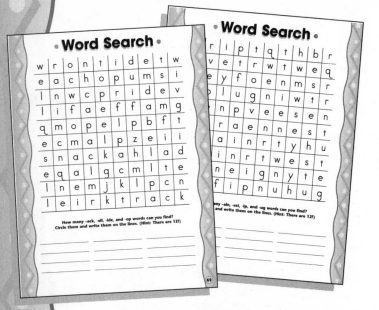

Search for Word Family Words (page 69–70)
Children search for word family words and circle them. You can also make your own word searches with any number of words you wish by using graph paper.

Word Family Bingo (page 71)
Have children randomly write a word family word (list 25–30 on the board) in each square. Then, call out words one at a time. Have children put a marker or color on the square with that word. The first child to get five across calls "bingo!" Children may also enjoy the leading the game.

Stationary (page 72)
Reproducible stationary for any writing activity!

Beyond the Practice Sheets

Extend word family learning beyond the practice pages and invite children to explore phonograms in a variety of ways! Here are a few ideas to get you started:

Word Family Riddles
Expand students' vocabulary with rhyming word family riddles. Solve the riddles as a class, or have students take turns solving them. Begin each riddle by saying a word with which the answer rhymes and end it by saying the answer's beginning sound. For example, say "This word rhymes with *dock* and starts with *cl*." If students need help, provide another word family clue, such as "This word also rhymes with *rock*." Or, offer a different kind of clue, such as "This word names a machine that tells time." Have students solve the riddle and identify the word family aloud ("The answer is *clock*. The word family is −ock.")

Matching Socks, Making Words
Help children explore word families by matching socks! Cut sock shapes from paper, eight to ten socks per word family. (To make this activity even more fun, ask parents to donate new white socks!) On one sock, write the word pattern the class is studying. On the other socks, write word beginnings—including consonants, blends, and digraphs. Place the socks in a laundry bag or basket and place it in a learning center. Invite students to work in pairs, placing socks next to each other and making word family words. Have children keep a list of words they've made. When students are ready to tackle more word families, add more word family socks and word-beginning socks.

Collaborative Posters
Celebrate student learning and decorate the classroom with word family posters made by students. You'll need one sheet of oaktag to make each word family poster. As a class, brainstorm word family words for each poster. Then divide the class into small groups. Have students use crayons and markers to illustrate the words on the posters. Or, provide magazines from which children can cut pictures.

Family-Style Concentration
Children match words in the same word family as they play this extra-fun version of concentration. To start, select three or four word families. (See the grid on page 5.) On a set of index cards, write one word family word per card. To play, children turn all the cards facedown and turn over two at a time, trying to match two words within the same word family. If they do so, they keep the cards and take another turn; if they do not, they turn the cards back over and the next player has a turn. For example, if a student turns over *play* and *tray* he or she has found a word family match. Both *play* and *tray* belong in the −ay word family. If a student turns over *play* and *snug* he or she has not found a match. The next player may take a turn.

Name: _____

The

─ack

family

Word Building

Put the letters together to make the -ack sound.

1. t + ack = _____

2. sh + ack = _____

3. s + ack = _____

4. tr + ack = _____

Sentence Fill-ins

Cut out the letters at the bottom of the page. Glue them in the correct squares to finish each sentence.

What did you ☐ack for lunch?

My shirt stripes are red and ☐ack.

He ate a ☐ack of pancakes.

I'm hungry for a ☐ack.

✂

| sn | bl | st | p |

Word Scramble

Unscramble each word. Write it on the line.

ktac _____

kpac _____

cksha _____

akblc _____

ksac _____

ackst _____

cktra _____

csnak _____

Word Search

Find and circle each word from the word bank.

a c s t a c k n h k c q u a c k c q s d
r k t a c k c k m v b l a c k c s d k f
d k s n a c k n p c k p a c k c r k w c
t c s h a c k c j k l c c b v m k s c q
s k s a c k c k r t t r a c k c e r k l
c b k r a c k c k c b v m k s d p l k m

Word Bank

black	shack
pack	snack
quack	stack
rack	tack
sack	track

More -ack Words

Write a sentence using one of the -ack family words.

_____

_____

_____

_____

Name: _____

Word Building
Put the letters together to make the -ail sound.

1. p + ail = _____

2. t + ail = _____

3. m + ail = _____

4. s + ail = _____

Sentence Fill-ins
Cut out the letters at the bottom of the page. Glue them in the correct squares to finish each sentence.

Let's hike up the ☐ail.

She looks weak and ☐ail.

I saw a ☐ail feather under a tree.

A ☐ail crawled on a leaf.

fr tr sn qu

Word Scramble

Unscramble each word. Write it on the line.

ilpa   ----------------------

lati   ----------------------

mlai   ----------------------

isal   ----------------------

tilra   ----------------------

afril   ----------------------

ansil   ----------------------

qauil   ----------------------

Word Search

Find and circle each word from the word bank.

```
u y v b l r p a i l r b l r a i l r j l
n b j k l s a i l r v b l g l w a i l y
a m s v b l f l t r a i l r k v b l p x
z i b f v c p r b l k l q u a i l r k l
e b l t y l s n a i l r f l m a i l x l
w l m b l t a i l r k l f r a i l r k l
```

Word Bank

frail   sail

mail   snail

pail   tail

quail   trail

rail   wail

More -ail Words

Write a sentence using one of the –ail family words.

Word Building

Put the letters together to make the -ain sound.

The

-ain

family

1. tr + ain = _____

2. ch + ain = _____

3. r + ain = _____

4. br + ain = _____

Sentence Fill-ins

Cut out the letters at the bottom of the page. Glue them in the correct squares to finish each sentence.

Water goes down the ☐ain.

There is a ☐ain on his new shirt.

Wheat is a kind of ☐ain.

When I broke my arm, I felt ☐ain.

st dr p gr

Word Scramble
Unscramble each word. Write it on the line.

aintr _____   drian _____

icnha _____   nstai _____

nira _____   ngrai _____

bairn _____   inpa _____

Word Search
Find and circle each word from the word bank.

t p y i v m a i n m n j n l b r a i n c

z i v p a i n w i l m b j n i l a j k l

a l s p r a i n y v c h a i n j n i l x

n i w i l m b a r i n i y i v d r a i n

i j a k p l g r a i n w l m b t r a i n

n z i r a i n y v s t a i n k n i j i l

Word Bank

brain   pain

chain   rain

drain   sprain

grain   stain

main   train

More -ain Words
Write a sentence using one of the -ain family words.

_____

_____

_____

_____

Word Building

Put the letters together to make the -ake sound.

1. r + ake = _____

2. c + ake = _____

3. sn + ake = _____

4. l + ake = _____

Sentence Fill-ins

Cut out the letters at the bottom of the page. Glue them in the correct squares to finish each sentence.

I ☐ ake my bed every morning.

Maria and Zach ☐ ake piano lessons.

Those ☐ ake flowers are made of silk.

They ☐ ake cookies in the oven.

t   f   m   b

Word Scramble

Unscramble each word. Write it on the line.

kera — — — — — — — —

amke — — — — — — — —

ckea — — — — — — — —

tkea — — — — — — — —

saken — — — — — — — —

feak — — — — — — — —

elka — — — — — — — —

kbae — — — — — — — —

Word Search

Find and circle each word from the word bank.

n k a z i r m k b t l a k e j k l a c v

x a m a k e j n z i r k l b a k e m k b

k j k a l s h a k e m k b n z i r a k t

s t a k e a m n a k z i r b t r a k e j

c a k e j n z i r k l t a k e m k b t k

m k b t s n a k e j n z i r k l f a k e

Word Bank

bake rake

cake shake

fake snake

lake stake

make take

More -ake Words

Write a sentence using one of the –ake family words.

_____

_____

_____

Name: _____

Word Building

Put the letters together to make the -ale sound.

1. wh + ale = _____

2. sc + ale = _____

3. s + ale = _____

4. b + ale = _____

Sentence Fill-ins

Cut out the letters at the bottom of the page. Glue them in the correct squares to finish each sentence.

Those potato chips taste ☐ale.

I know a fairy ☐ale about a swan.

He looked weak and ☐ale.

I like to eat ☐ale with carrots.

| k | st | p | t |

Word Scramble

Unscramble each word. Write it on the line.

waleh _ _ _ _ _ _ _ _ _ _ _ _ _ _ _   tleas _ _ _ _ _ _ _ _ _ _ _ _ _ _

sleca _ _ _ _ _ _ _ _ _ _ _ _ _ _   alet _ _ _ _ _ _ _ _ _ _ _ _ _ _ _

lesa _ _ _ _ _ _ _ _ _ _ _ _ _ _ _   lpae _ _ _ _ _ _ _ _ _ _ _ _ _ _ _

leab _ _ _ _ _ _ _ _ _ _ _ _ _ _ _   leka _ _ _ _ _ _ _ _ _ _ _ _ _ _ _

Word Search

Find and circle each word from the word bank.

j t l a k t a l e n z j k i r w h a l e
t l a s c a l e i n z i r m a l e e j k
e i j k p a l e n z e j k i r s a l e z
t l a k a l e e j k b a l e t l a x c v
n z i r t l a s t a l e n z i r g a l e
b j s f l e p t c o h p a k p c i h r f

Word Bank

bale   sale

gale   scale

kale   stale

male   tale

pale   whale

More -ale Words

Write a sentence using one of the –ale family words.

_ _

_ _

_ _

Name: _____

Word Building

Put the letters together to make the -an sound.

1. c + an = _____

2. f + an = _____

3. m + an = _____

4. p + an = _____

Sentence Fill-ins

Cut out the letters at the bottom of the page. Glue them in the correct squares to finish each sentence.

Her mother drives a blue ☐an.

We ☐an around the playground.

I like to eat ☐an muffins.

My foot is bigger ☐an your foot.

th v r br

Word Scramble

Unscramble each word. Write it on the line.

nca _____

nva _____

nfa _____

nra _____

anm _____

anbr _____

anp _____

hatn _____

Word Search

Find and circle each word from the word bank.

t x c v l n a r i h r t h a n e j k n a

e j k b r a n t l n a i h r k m a n h r

p a n e v n a j k f a n i h r n a p u y

n a i h r e j k s c a n t l a c a n i o

s n y t a n v i d n a s p a n e n a j k

t n a l a v a n e j n a k g a i h r a n

Word Bank

bran   ran

can   scan

fan   span

man   than

pan   van

More -an Words

Write a sentence using one of the -an family words.

_____

- -

_____

_____

Name: _____

Word Building
Put the letters together to make the -ank sound.

1. pl + ank = _____

2. b + ank = _____

3. t + ank = _____

4. cr + ank = _____

Sentence Fill-ins
Cut out the letters at the bottom of the page. Glue them in the correct squares to finish each sentence.

I ☐ank a glass of chocolate milk.

Fill in the ☐ank space with a word.

She gave the rope a ☐ank.

The cheese ☐ank, but tasted great.

y │ bl │ st │ dr

Word Scramble

Unscramble each word. Write it on the line.

nkpla ------ _____

ankdr ------ _____

ankb ------ _____

ktans ------ _____

ktan ------ _____

bklan ------ _____

canrk ------ _____

nkya ------ _____

Word Search

Find and circle each word from the word bank.

p r m b i n a t a n k i o h r s t a n k

c k l b n k d r a n k r n a r t y j h j

i l r b l a n k r i o n a c r a n k e w

k a y a n k i b k r c a r n k y u r k n

n k r n a f l a n k i c y x r p l a n k

u r k n a k b a n k r n i s a n k v a k

Word Bank

bank	plank
blank	sank
crank	stank
drank	tank
flank	yank

More -ank Words

Write a sentence using one of the –ank family words.

_____

_____

_____

Name: _____

Word Building

Put the letters together to make the -ap sound.

The

–ap

family

1. m + ap = _____

2. c + ap = _____

3. cl + ap = _____

4. n + ap = _____

Sentence Fill-ins

Cut out the letters at the bottom of the page. Glue them in the correct squares to finish each sentence.

We can ☐ap the present.

Step over the ☐ap.

Tree ☐ap runs in the spring.

My book bag has a ☐ap.

g | wr | str | s

Word Scramble

Unscramble each word. Write it on the line.

apm _____   wpra _____

pac _____   gpa _____

capl _____   pas _____

anp _____   trasp _____

Word Search

Find and circle each word from the word bank.

n a p p t y x d c r s a p k f g p f g p

p t x p c y r f g b n p d f r w r a p o

g a p x v c s t r a p r e f g c j k p g

p i v c s n a p p t y r c a p f g p p l

y h x b c p t y r c l a p p o c m f g p

r t y n t a p p t y r f g p m a p o v c

Word Bank

cap	sap
clap	snap
gap	strap
map	tap
nap	wrap

More -ap Words

Write a sentence using one of the -ap family words.

_____

_____

_____

_____

Name: _____

Word Building

Put the letters together to make the -ash sound.

1. tr + ash = _____

2. fl + ash = _____

3. c + ash = _____

4. s + ash = _____

Sentence Fill-ins

Cut out the letters at the bottom of the page. Glue them in the correct squares to finish each sentence.

Let's ☐ash those potatoes.

I put medicine on my itchy ☐ash.

Dad's belly flop made a ☐ash.

Did you hear cooking pans ☐ash?

m | cr | r | spl

Word Scramble

Unscramble each word. Write it on the line.

sthra _____   asmh _____

flhas _____   rhas _____

scha _____   hapssl _____

ssah _____   hcsra _____

Word Search

Find and circle each word from the word bank.

```
s p x f h f r a s h x s n a g p p s h f
p s h f s n p s h f s p l a s h p s h f
c r a s h f s h n a g p p s h f c a s h
d p s r h w s a s h i r c m a s h i b v
s t a s h f g i s n a p t r a s h d s f
f g p f l a s h s n i a s m a s h b j k
```

Word Bank

cash   sash

crash   smash

flash   splash

mash   stash

rash   trash

More -ash Words

Write a sentence using one of the -ash family words.

_____

- -

_____

_____

Name: _____

Word Building

Put the letters together to make the -at sound.

1. c + at = _____

2. b + at = _____

3. r + at = _____

4. h + at = _____

Sentence Fill-ins

Cut out the letters at the bottom of the page. Glue them in the correct squares to finish each sentence.

Humpty Dumpty ☐at on a wall.

It was as ☐at as a pancake.

I like to ☐at on the telephone.

He coughed and ☐at out a gnat.

fl | s | sp | ch

Word Scramble

Unscramble each word. Write it on the line.

t c a _____   a t s _____

a t b _____   l a f t _____

t r a _____   c a h t _____

t a h _____   s a p t _____

Word Search

Find and circle each word from the word bank.

```
b j t t k b a t p s h f c h a t x t d t
s p a t h y t f l a t y r t y v b n t m
p s t h t f b j k s d f v t s g j t y t
b t j t k m a t b t v b y n j k t y j k
s l a t b j k h a t s a t p m l p s t h
t p s t t h f c a t b t j t k r a t t b
```

More -at Words

Write a sentence using one of the -at family words.

_____

_____

_____

_____

Name: _____

Word Building

Put the letters together to make the -ay sound.

1. h + ay = _____

2. j + ay = _____

3. cl + ay = _____

4. tr + ay = _____

Sentence Fill-ins

Cut out the letters at the bottom of the page. Glue them in the correct squares to finish each sentence.

We sailed across the ☐ ay.

My coat has ☐ ay buttons.

Branches ☐ way in the wind.

That fabric has begun to ☐ ay.

fr | sw | gr | b

Word Scramble

Unscramble each word. Write it on the line.

hya _____

yja _____

alyc _____

tyra _____

bya _____

ragy _____

yfra _____

sawy _____

Word Search

Find and circle each word from the word bank.

```
t y a b j k p l a y t c y a h h f m n o
y l a j a y t h f y a f r a y a r s t v
s y i e p y a x f v y a h s a y p e y a
c y a h b j k h a y t y a h f g r a y t
y a s w a y s y a p y x y i f o h b a y
c y a b j k h c l a y t h c h f t r a y
```

Word Bank

bay   jay

clay   play

fray   say

gray   sway

hay   tray

More -ay Words

Write a sentence using one of the -ay family words.

_____

_____

_____

_____

Name: _____

The
-ell
family

Word Building
Put the letters together to make the -ell sound.

1. b + ell = _____

2. sh + ell = _____

3. w + ell = _____

4. y + ell = _____

Sentence Fill-ins
Cut out the letters at the bottom of the page. Glue them in the correct squares to finish each sentence.

Jack and Jill ☐ell down the hill.

I can ☐ell really long words.

Can you ☐ell cookies baking?

We ☐ell lemonade in the summer.

s sm f sp

Word Scramble

Unscramble each word. Write it on the line.

lbel   _____

lfel   _____

lhels   _____

lspel   _____

llwe   _____

elsml   _____

lyel   _____

lsel   _____

Word Search

Find and circle each word from the word bank.

```
s e l l s r p c e l h e r f r s m e l l
p x d y c h f h c e l l t r y d h e l r
e s h e l l u y v e l b l d e l l b j k
t e l h f w e l l u y r d v e l b p d l
l e y e l l u r y d e l b r l s p e l l
b j k f e l l u r y e l b l b e l l t f
```

Word Bank

bell	shell
cell	smell
dell	spell
fell	well
sell	yell

More -ell Words

Write a sentence using one of the –ell family words.

_____

- -

_____

_____

Name: _____

Word Building

Put the letters together to make the -est sound.

1. v + est = _____

2. n + est = _____

3. ch + est = _____

4. p + est = _____

Sentence Fill-ins

Cut out the letters at the bottom of the page. Glue them in the correct squares to finish each sentence.

He is tired. He needs to ☐ est.

Do your ☐ est work.

Travel east, not ☐ est.

I'm ready to take the ☐ est.

b   r   w   t

Word Scramble

Unscramble each word. Write it on the line.

svet _____

tnes _____

hcste _____

espt _____

estt _____

esbt _____

stre _____

stwe _____

Word Search

Find and circle each word from the word bank.

u c y h b t j k y v b l t e s t t h s f

s t b e s t u y t v b l w e s t b j i k

t c h h f z e s t s p c h x f h r e s t

q u e s t u y v c h b l v e s t s t m b

b t j k n e s t s p x c h f h c h e s t

u s t b y h s t b v b l p e s t t f s t

Word Bank

best	rest
chest	test
nest	vest
pest	west
quest	zest

More -est Words

Write a sentence using one of the -est family words.

_____

_____

_____

Name: _____

Word Building
Put the letters together to make the -ice sound.

1. m + ice = _____

2. pr + ice = _____

3. d + ice = _____

4. r + ice = _____

Sentence Fill-ins
Cut out the letters at the bottom of the page. Glue them in the correct squares to finish each sentence.

Pepper is a ☐ ice.

He ate a ☐ ice of pizza.

Kind is another word for ☐ ice.

The phone rang ☐ ice.

sl | tw | sp | n

Word Scramble

Unscramble each word. Write it on the line.

emic   _____

icesl   _____

icpre   _____

neic   _____

cdie   _____

tcwie   _____

ecri   _____

cspie   _____

Word Search

Find and circle each word from the word bank.

```
b j k t w i c e s p x f h n i c e t h f
o t h c h f s p i c e u y v b l m i c e
e i c p r i c e s p x c h f i c h b j k
d i c e u y v b l t h r i c e t h i c f
i r i c e s p x f c h i c h s p l i c e
u e i c y v c h b l s l i c e b j k i c
```

Word Bank

dice   slice

mice   spice

nice   splice

price   thrice

rice   twice

More –ice Words

Write a sentence using one of the –ice family words.

_____

_____

_____

Name: _____

Word Building
Put the letters together to make the -ick sound.

1. s + ick= _____

2. k + ick= _____

3. ch + ick= _____

4. p + ick= _____

Sentence Fill-ins
Cut out the letters at the bottom of the page. Glue them in the correct squares to finish each sentence.

He likes to ⬚ ick lollipops.

The magic ⬚ ick was amazing.

Grass gets ⬚ ick when it rains.

The pond ice is two feet ⬚ ick.

| sl | l | tr | th |

Word Scramble

Unscramble each word. Write it on the line.

skic _____   kicl _____

ckik _____   icslk _____

kchic _____   tkhic _____

cpik _____   ktric _____

Word Search

Find and circle each word from the word bank.

```
e u y c k v c h b l k i c k t h c e k f
b j k t r i c k s p x f h q u i c k c k
u y v b l w i c k u y v b l c h i c k w
c k p i c k s p c h c k x f h s l i c k
t f h l i c k u c h y v b c k l s i c k
s p c c k h x f h t h i c k b c k j k h
```

Word Bank

chick sick

kick slick

lick thick

pick trick

quick wick

More -ick Words

Write a sentence using one of the -ick family words.

_____

_____

_____

Name: _____

Word Building

Put the letters together to make the -ide sound.

1. sl + ide = _____

2. r + ide = _____

3. h + ide = _____

4. t + ide = _____

Sentence Fill-ins

Cut out the letters at the bottom of the page. Glue them in the correct squares to finish each sentence.

The box landed on its ☐ide.

They ☐ide on their ice skates.

We take ☐ide in doing homework.

The ☐ide wore a lace gown.

gl | pr | s | br

Word Scramble

Unscramble each word. Write it on the line.

dslie _____   idse _____

erid _____   dglie _____

idhe _____   riedp _____

teid _____   debri _____

Word Search

Find and circle each word from the word bank.

b i d j k t c p h e c t d o f g l i d e

p r i d e s p x i d c h e f h b r i d e

s l i d e u i y e v b l i d h i d e i d

u y i d c h v b e l t i d e b j e i d k

t h i d f s i d e b j s p h s t r i d e

i n s i d e s p x c e i d h f h r i d e

Word Bank

bride   ride

glide   side

hide   slide

inside stride

pride   tide

More –ide Words

Write a sentence using one of the –ide family words.

_____

_____

_____

Name: _____

Word Building

Put the letters together to make the -ight sound.

1. fl + ight = _____

2. kn + ight = _____

3. f + ight = _____

4. l + ight = _____

Sentence Fill-ins

Cut out the letters at the bottom of the page. Glue them in the correct squares to finish each sentence.

The scary mask gave me a ☐ight.

We ☐ight go on a vacation in July.

The ☐ight lamp hurt my eyes.

His shoes were too ☐ight.

| t | fr | m | br |

Word Scramble
Unscramble each word. Write it on the line.

htgfli _____ fgriht _____

igtknh _____ htmig _____

htfig _____ thlig _____

slhigt _____ httig _____

Word Search
Find and circle each word from the word bank.

```
f l i g h t s p c b j k h m i g h t f h
t s i h i d f d e b j s p h s d e t r i
u y b l s i g h t t h f k n i g h t h g
f i g h t s p c b j k h x f h t i g h t
t h f r i g h t u y v b c l i g h t h t
c s l i g h t h v h f s r i g h t u t y
```

Word Bank

fight	might
flight	right
fright	sight
knight	slight
light	tight

More –ight Words
Write a sentence using one of the –ight family words.

_____

_____

_____

_____

Name: _____

The

-ill

family

Word Building

Put the letters together to make the -ill sound.

1. b + ill = _____

2. h + ill = _____

3. dr + ill = _____

4. gr + ill = _____

Sentence Fill-ins

Cut out the letters at the bottom of the page. Glue them in the correct squares to finish each sentence.

We ☐ill ride the roller coaster.

The cool wind gave me a ☐ill.

That ☐ill is from a porcupine.

Put the plant on a window ☐ill.

s | w | qu | ch

Word Scramble

Unscramble each word. Write it on the line.

blil _____   lwil _____

lhil _____   liqul _____

ildrl _____   lichl _____

irlgl _____   lsil _____

Word Search

Find and circle each word from the word bank.

```
t c l h l h f q u i l l s p x f h t h f
c h i l l u y l l b l h i l l t h f h l
c x f h d r i l l t h h f g r i l l s p
s i l l s l p l f c l h h b i l l j k y
t l h f w i l l u c b v b l t h r i l l
u l b l j k y v l c l h l b l m i l l u
```

More -ill Words

Write a sentence using one of the –ill family words.

_____

_____

_____

Name: _____

The
−in
family

Word Building
Put the letters together to make the -in sound.

1. ch + in = _____

2. tw + in = _____

3. p + in = _____

4. f + in = _____

Sentence Fill-ins
Cut out the letters at the bottom of the page. Glue them in the correct squares to finish each sentence.

Sam wants to ☐in the race.

Let's ☐in the top again.

The ball hit me on the ☐in.

A ☐in is a kind of smile.

gr sh sp w

Word Scramble
Unscramble each word. Write it on the line.

hinc _____

inw _____

itwn _____

pnsi _____

npi _____

snhi _____

nfi _____

igrn _____

Word Search
Find and circle each word from the word bank.

```
u y n c b j k h n i v b l s p i n t h f
t h n f s h i n s p x f h c h i n r e t
n t w i n t h n f p i n z x i z b b c b
f i n s p b j k x c h f h g r i n t h f
u n y v t i n b c n h l r t i i w i n r
t h f s k i n u y n c n i m i h v n b l
```

Word Bank

chin	skin
fin	spin
grin	tin
pin	twin
shin	win

More -in Words
Write a sentence using one of the -in family words.

_____

_____

_____

Name: _____

Word Building

Put the letters together to make the -ine sound.

1. p + ine = _____

2. l + ine = _____

3. v + ine = _____

4. n + ine = _____

Sentence Fill-ins

Cut out the letters at the bottom of the page. Glue them in the correct squares to finish each sentence.

I can see the sun ☐ine.

Pigs are also called ☐ine.

☐ine is thicker than thread.

The ☐ine is made of bones.

sh sw t w sp

Word Scramble

Unscramble each word. Write it on the line.

inep _____

neli _____

envi _____

nnie _____

nishe _____

snewi _____

netwi _____

epnsi _____

Word Search

Find and circle each word from the word bank.

```
t b j n i k h f s w i n e u y v n i b l
u c h y v b l s p i n e t h f p i n e w
t n i h f l i n e s p x n i f h v i n e
u t y n i c n i h v b l t w i n e b j k
b j k m i n e s p x f n i h f i n e n i
t h x f s h i n e u y c h v b l n i n e
```

Word Bank

fine	shine
line	spine
mine	swine
nine	twine
pine	vine

More –ine Words

Write a sentence using one of the –ine family words.

_____

_____

_____

Name: _____

The **-ing** family

Word Building

Put the letters together to make the -ing sound.

1. k + ing = _____

2. w + ing = _____

3. r + ing = _____

4. sw + ing = _____

Sentence Fill-ins

Cut out the letters at the bottom of the page. Glue them in the correct squares to finish each sentence.

Tie the ☐ing in a knot.

When bees ☐ing, it hurts.

I ☐ing in the chorus.

My broken arm is in a ☐ing.

| sl | s | st | str |

Word Scramble

Unscramble each word. Write it on the line.

r g i n _____

i g n s t r _____

g k n i _____

g s i n _____

s i g n w _____

g s n l i _____

g i n w _____

n s g t i _____

Word Search

Find and circle each word from the word bank.

t n b n g j n g k h f r i n g t h n g f

n k i n g s p b j k c h x f h s l i n g

u y c h v b l s t i n g f l i n g v b l

t h f t h i n g s p x f h s w i n g r t

g n w i n g u y v n g b l s t r i n g g

s p x f n g b j k h s i n g t h c g h f

Word Bank

fling   sting

king   string

ring   swing

sing   thing

sling   wing

More -ing Words

Write a sentence using one of the -ing family words.

_____

- -

_____

_____

Name: _____

Word Building
Put the letters together to make the -ink sound.

1. s + ink = _____

2. w + ink = _____

3. dr + ink = _____

4. l + ink = _____

Sentence Fill-ins
Cut out the letters at the bottom of the page. Glue them in the correct squares to finish each sentence.

He goes skating at the ☐ink.

We use our brains to ☐ink.

Those skunks in our yard ☐ink.

Her favorite color is ☐ink.

| p | r | r | st | th |

Word Scramble

Unscramble each word. Write it on the line.

sikn _____   rnki _____

knwi _____   hkint _____

dknri _____   nstki _____

nlik _____   kinp _____

Word Search

Find and circle each word from the word bank.

```
s p x f h t h i n k t h f s t i n k y l
r e p i n k s p x f h s i n k t h c h f
t h f w i n k u y v b j k c h b n k i y
d r i n k s p b j k h s h r i n k t h f
u y v b j k b l s l i n k t h f l i n k
k b n k j k t h f r i n k s p x f n k h
```

Word Bank

drink	sink
link	slink
pink	stink
rink	think
shrink	wink

More –ink Words

Write a sentence using one of the –ink family words.

_____

_____

_____

_____

Name: _____

Word Building
Put the letters together to make the -ip sound.

1. sh + ip = _____

2. dr + ip = _____

3. r + ip = _____

4. ch + ip = _____

Sentence Fill-ins
Cut out the letters at the bottom of the page. Glue them in the correct squares to finish each sentence.

The gymnast did a ☐ip.

Pack your suitcase for the ☐ip.

Barbers use scissors to ☐ip hair.

Please ☐ip a bat with both hands.

gr | sn | fl | tr

Word Scramble

Unscramble each word. Write it on the line.

fpli _____

ciph _____

spni _____

ptir _____

rdip _____

rpig _____

pri _____

ipsh _____

Word Search

Find and circle each word from the word bank.

```
t r i p s p x f s p h g r i p t s h i p
r i u i p y v b l d r i p t s p h r i f
t r r i p s b j p r i k p x s p f r i h
t r i h f c h i p u c h y v b l w h i p
e r s l i p s p b j k x r i c h r i f h
t h f f l i p u y b j k c v b l s n i p
```

Word Bank

chip   ship

drip   slip

flip   snip

grip   trip

rip . whip

More -ip Words

Write a sentence using one of the -ip family words.

_____

_____

_____

_____

The

–ock

family

Word Building

Put the letters together to make the -ock sound.

1. r + ock= _____

2. s + ock= _____

3. cl + ock= _____

4. d + ock= _____

Sentence Fill-ins

Cut out the letters at the bottom of the page. Glue them in the correct squares to finish each sentence.

Put on a ☐ ock before you paint.

A ☐ ock of geese flew South.

Did you hear a ☐ ock at the door?

We need to ☐ ock the gate.

l kn fl sm

Word Scramble

Unscramble each word. Write it on the line.

crko _____

kfcol _____

skoc _____

okknc _____

cosmk _____

cclok _____

olkc _____

dkoc _____

Word Search

Find and circle each word from the word bank.

```
s p b j k x f h r o c k u c h y u v b l
l o c k u y c k v c k b l f l o c k i y
t h c k b j k h f k n o c k t h c k i f
f r o c k s p x b j k f h s o c k t h f
c l o c k t c h h c k f d o c k x f c k
t b j k h f c r o c k s p h s m o c k k
```

Word Bank

clock   knock

crock   lock

dock   rock

flock   smock

frock   sock

More -ock Words

Write a sentence using one of the -ock family words.

_____

_____

_____

Name: _____

Word Building
Put the letters together to make the -op sound.

1. t + op = _____

2. st + op = _____

3. m + op = _____

4. c + op = _____

Sentence Fill-ins
Cut out the letters at the bottom of the page. Glue them in the correct squares to finish each sentence.

He can ☐op wood with an axe.

Let's ☐op like rabbits.

The farmer had a ☐op of corn.

We ☐op at the mall.

| cr | sh | h | ch |

Word Scramble

Unscramble each word. Write it on the line.

opst _____ opc _____

hosp _____ pto _____

pho _____ hocp _____

porc _____ omp _____

Word Search

Find and circle each word from the word bank.

b j k t o p t h f s c h p x f h p l o p
c o p s p x c h f h m o p b j k i o p t
t c h h f s t o p u y v o p b l c h o p
p o c r o p s p x f h s h o p b o j k
c h p u y v b l h o p o c p e h i p y o
b j k f l o p t c o h p m k p c i h h f

More –op Words

Write a sentence using one of the –op family words.

_____

_____

_____

_____

The
-ot
family

Word Building
Put the letters together to make the -ot sound.

1. p + ot = _____

2. kn + ot = _____

3. h + ot = _____

4. c + ot = _____

Sentence Fill-ins
Cut out the letters at the bottom of the page. Glue them in the correct squares to finish each sentence.

Horses ☐ot and gallop.

There is a ☐ot on your clean dress.

He went to the doctor for a ☐ot.

A ☐ot is another word for child.

✂

| t | sh | tr | sp |

Word Scramble

Unscramble each word. Write it on the line.

tpo _____   ttro _____

oktn _____   tosp _____

tho _____   soht _____

tco _____   tto _____

Word Search

Find and circle each word from the word bank.

```
u w u y o t v b l t r o t s p x o t f h
y i s p o t b j k b h t o t c h o t h f
s p w c b h o x t f h t t o b j k c o t
o t s h o t k l b y w p t o t i p l o t
b j b k j o t s p c h x b f h p o t u y
u o t y w o t v b l l b l k n o t l k g
```

Word Bank

cot	pot
hot	shot
jot	spot
knot	tot
plot	trot

More -ot Words

Write a sentence using one of the –ot family words.

_____

_____

_____

Name: _____

Word Building

Put the letters together to make the -uck sound.

1. d + uck = _____

2. b + uck = _____

3. tr + uck = _____

4. cl + uck = _____

Sentence Fill-ins

Cut out the letters at the bottom of the page. Glue them in the correct squares to finish each sentence.

Pass the hockey ☐uck to me!

That penny will give you ☐uck.

My mom will ☐uck me in tonight.

His shoe was ☐uck in the mud.

p   t   l   st

Word Scramble

Unscramble each word. Write it on the line.

kcdu _____

cpku _____

uklc _____

kctu _____

stukc _____

bkuc _____

kutrc _____

kcucl _____

Word Search

Find and circle each word from the word bank.

```
b j k d u c k t s p x c h f h p l u c k
r r u y c k v c k b c k l b n m b u c k
t r u c k s p c k x u f h p u c k b j k
u c k c h c k v c k b l u l u c k k l m
u i p c l u c k s p x c k f u h t u c k
b u j u k s t u c k t h u c h i m u c k
```

Word Bank

buck	pluck
cluck	puck
duck	stuck
luck	truck
muck	tuck

More -uck Words

Write a sentence using one of the –uck family words.

_____

_____

_____

-ug

Name: _____

Word Building

Put the letters together to make the –ug sound.

1. h + ug = _____

2. m + ug = _____

3. j + ug = _____

4. b + ug = _____

Sentence Fill-ins

Cut out the letters at the bottom of the page. Glue them in the correct squares to finish each sentence.

I ☐ug in the sand with a shovel.

Blankets keep us warm and ☐ug.

He gave the string a ☐ug.

Let's ☐ug the hole.

pl d sn t

Word Scramble

Unscramble each word. Write it on the line.

nsug _____   jgu _____

pglu _____   utg _____

mgu _____   udg _____

ugh _____   bgu _____

Word Search

Find and circle each word from the word bank.

```
g h j t u g l p w r t y o p l g l b u g
u h j r k p l d u g c v b j u g x c b g
r u g x y z n b n m p l u g o g q w s u
v b n s d w e i p x c x s x c m u g d y
z r t y w e r t s m u g w d i w b n b g
i h u g l m p o r t q m u h y j s n u g
```

Word Bank

bug   plug

dug   rug

hug   smug

jug   snug

mug   tug

More -ug Words

Write a sentence using one of the –ug family words.

_____

_____

_____

_____

Word Building

Put the letters together to make the -ump sound.

1. st + ump = _____

2. h + ump = _____

3. j + ump = _____

4. gr + ump = _____

Sentence Fill-ins

Cut out the letters at the bottom of the page. Glue them in the correct squares to finish each sentence.

Don't [ ]ump your head!

Use the [ ]ump to fill the bucket.

The pumpkin was round and [ ]ump.

Trash is stored at a [ ]ump.

p | b | pl | d

Word Scramble

Unscramble each word. Write it on the line.

mpbu _____

mphu _____

rupmg _____

ppum _____

pjum _____

muppl _____

umpst _____

mpdu _____

Word Search

Find and circle each word from the word bank.

```
u y c h v b l s t u m p s p x p l u m p
f h u m p u c h y v f h b l j u m p p m
o p g m h b u m p m p c h g r u m p s t
j s d b n h k m p p u m p s p m p x f h
d u m p t h c h f c l u m p w s p x f h
t c m p e r c a b t h j k h h f l u m p
```

Word Bank

bump	jump
clump	lump
dump	plump
grump	pump
hump	stump

More -ump Words

Write a sentence using one of the -ump family words.

_____

_____

_____

_____

Name: _____

Word Building
Put the letters together to make the -unk sound.

1. sk + unk = _____

2. tr + unk = _____

3. b + unk = _____

4. s + unk = _____

Sentence Fill-ins
Cut out the letters at the bottom of the page. Glue them in the correct squares to finish each sentence.

She made a slam ☐ unk at the game.

May I have a ☐ unk of candy?

This shirt is too small. It ☐ unk.

The skunk sprayed. The air ☐ unk.

shr | st | d | ch

Word Scramble

Unscramble each word. Write it on the line.

ntrku _____

nkbu _____

uhcnk _____

knsrhu _____

knksu _____

uskn _____

trkun _____

nskut _____

Word Search

Find and circle each word from the word bank.

```
m n s k u n k s p x h h u n k s p x f h
h k v b l t r u n k m n u y i c n b h
k n k m s u n k s p x f h b u n k k m n
u y c h b l s t u n k s p k x f h n j k
k j u n k t h f d u n k k m p x n k m n
m n c h u n k u y c h l c h s h r u n k
```

Word Bank

bunk	shrunk
chunk	skunk
dunk	stunk
hunk	sunk
junk	trunk

More -unk Words

Write a sentence using one of the -unk family words.

_____

_____

_____

• Word Search •

w	r	o	n	t	i	d	e	t	w
e	a	c	h	o	p	u	m	s	i
l	n	w	c	p	r	i	d	e	v
l	i	f	a	e	f	f	a	m	g
q	m	o	p	e	l	p	b	f	t
e	c	m	a	l	p	z	e	i	i
s	n	a	c	k	a	h	l	a	d
e	q	a	l	g	c	m	l	t	e
l	n	e	m	j	k	l	p	c	n
l	e	i	r	k	t	r	a	c	k

How many –ack, -ell, -ide, and -op words can you find?
Circle them and write them on the lines. (Hint: There are 12!)

_____ _____ _____

_____ _____ _____

_____ _____ _____

_____ _____ _____

Word Search

t	r	i	p	t	q	t	h	b	r
u	v	e	t	r	w	t	w	e	q
g	e	y	f	o	e	n	m	s	r
e	p	l	u	g	n	i	w	t	r
o	e	n	p	v	e	e	s	e	n
t	e	r	a	e	n	n	e	s	t
s	t	a	i	n	r	t	y	h	u
n	e	i	n	r	t	w	e	s	t
i	t	n	e	i	g	n	y	t	e
p	e	f	i	p	n	u	h	u	g

How many –ain, -est, -ip, and -ug words can you find?
Circle them and write them on the lines. (Hint: There are 12!)

_____   _____   _____

_____   _____   _____

_____   _____   _____

_____

Word Family Bingo

		★		